THE UNDERPINNINGS OF AMERICAN FOREIGN POLICY

I face the world as it is, and cannot stand idle in the face of threats to the American people. For make no mistake: Evil does exist in the world. A non-violent movement could not have halted Hitler's armies. Negotiations cannot convince al Qaeda's leaders to lay down their arms. To say that force may sometimes be necessary is not a call to cynicism -- it is recognition of history; the imperfections of man and the limits of reason.

—President Barrack Obama,
Nobel Acceptance Speech, December 10th, 2009.

President Obama's Nobel Peace Prize acceptance speech in December, 2009, dismayed many of his liberal constituents and surprised his conservative opponents.   In war-like terms, similar to his predecessor, he defended his right as the commander in chief to use military force and if necessary act unilaterally in the face of terrorism. He firmly stated what all United States Presidents are thereby sworn; to the best of their ability they must "preserve, protect and defend the Constitution of the United States" and by extension, the interests and welfare of its citizenry. President Obama's articulated, albeit hotly debated by his critics, a reasoned acknowledgement that we do not live in a utopian world. His strategic message was clear; President Obama defended his obligation to first protect American vital national interests, and second; as the leader of the world's only remaining super power, the additional responsibility to protect "global goods" and vital international interests. As he accepted the Nobel Peace Prize, he set the tone for his foreign policy; interventionist when necessary, continuing a theme first articulated by Woodrow Wilson and actively pursued by every president since.

In response to President Obama's speech, particularly those dismayed and surprised of his subsequent decision to surge ground troops in Afghanistan, this paper will explore the origins, underpinnings and evolution of United States foreign policy. As reviewed in this paper's thesis, American foreign policy is derived from our values and national experience, and its distinct and unique underpinnings rooted in the history and psychology of early American colonists and its founding fathers. American Presidents' across the political spectrum have consistently centered their foreign policy decisions based on American values and experience. We should therefore, not be surprised to find, that as politically dissimilar Presidents Bush and Obama are, they have made remarkably similar foreign policy decisions when faced with global terrorism and attacks on the homeland.

First, this paper will explore the underpinnings of American Foreign Policy. Is it intrinsically founded on our national identity, values and culture? Second, this paper the will address the evolution brought on by America's intervention and participation in the two World Wars; and what aspects of our America heritage and values explain our Interventionalism and desire to spread democracy. In conclusion, this paper's analysis will examine President Obama's two recent speeches; first his Nobel Peace Prize acceptance speech where he articulated his foreign policy; and second, his speech at the Unites States Military Academy at West Point, where he followed his rhetoric with decision to surge troops in Afghanistan. His rhetoric and decision should not have surprised either liberals or foreign policy hawks. His decision was a predictable, based on the evolution of American foreign policy, and the limits by which our values and national experience binds the Presidential foreign policy decisions in protecting our vital national interests.

<u>The Early American Experience; Underpinnings of American Foreign Policy</u>

Early Americans migrated from many regions of Europe, but for the most part were English in lineage and culture. Many of the original colonists were Puritans who having fled the volatile political environment of 17th century England, established colonies in North America, later the United States of America. Puritans had a deep-rooted distrust of British power. The English rulers and clergy had created a hostile religious and political climate, motivating Puritans and other groups to leave England and establish colonies elsewhere. They desired the geographic separation, economic and religious freedom, if not isolation from the English resulting in the Great Migration and the subsequent founding of the Massachusetts Bay Colony and other settlements. But Puritan economic, religious and individual aspirations were offset by fear, insecurity and isolation as they found themselves separated both geographically and philosophically from their English heritage. This geographic isolation of America provided distinct benefits, protecting the early colonists from European entanglements and the ravages of war. The Puritan and colonial separation and their rejection of English rule created the fundamental values that permeated colonial domestic and foreign policy.

Puritans' considered hard work a proponent of a person's calling, if not moral obligation. The Puritan ethic prescribed worldly success as a sign of personal salvation. Individual and collective industrial might, property rights, and free-trade are Puritan legacies and key attributes of the capitalistic nature of United States domestic and foreign policy.[1] The Puritan ethic is observed in the meddling aspects of United States domestic and foreign policy. The requirement of "right living" has lead to the more fanatical and dogmatic aspect of American individual and national identity.[2] Their story of seeking religious freedom, independent thought, and hard work has become a central theme of the history and culture of the United States.

The impact of this geographic separation and security cannot be over-exaggerated in the formulation of America's sense of uniqueness, independence and early isolation.[3] The American colonists were the only major state in the world at that time without direct and aggressive powerful neighbors. From a distance Americans would criticize but retain many aspects of their European and English culture. They would reject intrusive European forms of government, and their religious overtones. Early Americans developed a sense of individual and collective freedom, removed from the necessity of direct interaction and diplomacy. Early Puritans and successive waves of immigrants created a society and culture based on the novel principles of social, economic and political organization.[4] American colonists, unencumbered by European and British influences succeeded in creating a definitive American culture with values rooted in their early pilgrim experience.

America's early foreign policy supported its domestic and expansionist policy, particularly as colonist developed trading and commercial relationships with the European continent. As America expanded, Puritan influence waned, replaced by a broad-based commercial and mercantile interest. Colonial success in migrating west further developed a sense of national adventure and self-reliance. American notions of national uniqueness and willingness, if not aggressiveness in taking on difficult tasks was then and as seen in our interventionist policies are a byproduct of this frontier mentality.

America's commercial and capitalist underpinnings began as colonial merchants expanded economically and began trading in earnest with the British. Americans benefited from an abundance of cultivable soil, water and minerals and combined with an energetic and growing population created a culture and society growing far faster than its ability to effectively govern.[5] The British promoted American expansion, but increasingly saw the colony as a source of revenue, instituting tariffs and taxes not representative of their contribution to the colony's common defense, and in opposition to colonial ingenuity and labor. As American commercial and trade expanded, British merchants began to resent and fear colonial competition. British merchants successfully petitioned the British government for not only favorable commercial protections, but additionally, British governance of the colonies. Initially Americans, in good faith, accepted British sovereignty in exchange for commercial partnership and military protection. And for the most part, British sovereigns, recognizing America's isolated geography, allowed American colonists some measure of political autonomy.

Significant rifts emerged as the British subordinated colonial interests to their commercial and imperial objectives. As the frontier wars ended in 1763, colonial leaders, powerful landowners and growing numbers of merchants and farmers, saw little need for continued British governance and military support. The British, with some logic, believed they had provided a significant military and commercial benefit in exchange for their colonial rule. English commercial continued to suffer. American merchants, leveraging their abundant resources, expanded and competed directly with British commerce. King George III, responding to commercial interests, tightened his control on the colonies. He established laws protecting British commerce, notably the

1765 the Stamp Act, instituting tariffs on Colonial exports and commercial taxes targeting American merchants. In addition to protecting British commercial interests, King George required hard cash to pay off war debts seen has having protected the colonies from French and Native Americans rivals.

The British resented American disinterest in their European affairs. They viewed colonial autonomy and independence in some measure as ungrateful arrogance. European culture and economic wealth had been a result of eighteen hundred years of gradual economic growth, interrupted frequently by feudal and intersectional war. Continental governments of the era habitually worked in concert with friendly nations to collectively attain their political and economic goals. Americans felt no obligation to support British interests outside of their immediate colonial sphere. Americans instead relied on geographic distance and abundant natural resources to advance their security and domestic needs. The Colonists rebuffed British expansionist interests; seen as increasingly dangerous as the French expanded in concert on the North American continent. American colonists, without imperial interests, pragmatically saw the French and, for the most part, the Spanish as expansionist competitors rather than military threats.

In the years leading up to America's independence, colonist bitterness came to a head. The colonists reviled the King's taxes and the heavy handed domestic tactics. Colonial leadership, representing a coalition of the elites from the original thirteen colonies, coalesced as a united political body; the Continental Congress. Patrick Henry's absolutist terms, "Give me Liberty or Give me Death" provided the moral impetus, whereby America's first governmental body agreed to reject British rule by military means. Recognizing America's geographic isolation, colonial leaders created the Continental Army, augmented throughout the war by colonial militia. They appointed George Washington as the first Commander-in-Chief. With his leadership, and significant financial and moral support from the French and the colonial population, the small but resilient United States military defeated a substantially better lead and equipped British regular army.

The success of the revolution was a defining moment in America's national experience. Having defeated the British, a major European power, Americans were convinced they were a unique and exceptional people, willing and able to accomplish great deeds. But more importantly, colonist desired little assistance and foreign involvement as the conducted domestic and foreign affairs.[6] America's early leaders, particularly its founding fathers and early presidents developed the underpinnings of foreign policy built on the unique aspects of American culture and experience. United States political populism and unilateralism were established by America's early rejection of British rule, Europe culture, and enlightenment. What early American diplomats may have attributed to astute foreign policy, may very likely just been the good fortune of being so far removed for powerful and greedy neighbors.

Over a twelve year period, following the Declaration of the Independence American leaders debated the Constitution. They rejected European forms of governance, but retained aspects of the English tort law; those supporting the colonial tenants of individual liberty an economic prosperity. George Washington and Thomas Jefferson argued against oppressive central government and foreign ties with the British. Jefferson insisted in his first inaugural address the view of "peace, commerce, and honest friendship with all nations, and entangling alliances with none."[7] America would instead focus inwardly on building the nation; avoiding foreign treaties and the entanglements in European wars.[8] Their common culture and heritage would become paramount in their debates of constitutional rights, individual liberty, prosperity, states' rights and union. The Constitution based on America's values, heritage and experience, as a statement governance, provided the basis for their present day and domestic and foreign policy.

Walter Reed Mead describes in his book, *Special Providence* four uniquely American foreign policy traditions, linked ostensibly with American history and culture.[9] Jeffersonians are non-interventionists, if not isolationists; the protectors of civil rights, suspicious of "entangling alliances." Persuaded that America's unique revolutionary heritage was a model to be emulated, they insisted that meddling in other nations' affairs served little purpose. Hamiltonians are economic nationalists who believe in enterprise at home and intervention aboard in support of commerce and economic national interests. Jacksonians, representing America's populist and nationalist sense of purpose, are committed to defending America's honor and national interests, often though the application of military power. Wilsonians are idealistic internationalists who advocate America's moral duty to spread democratic values abroad, defining American national interests in broad, international terms.[10] While Walter Mead's characterizations may over-simplify realist, pacifist, militaristic and international foreign policies, his association of these broader methods in the context of American culture and heritage provides a uniquely American understanding of United States foreign policy as it has evolved.

The Jeffersonian Tradition; Principled Isolationism

The Jeffersonian tradition, based on the political philosophy America's third President , called for a foreign policy predominantly in support of its domestic policy, particularly its constitutionally mandated civil liberties and the rule of law. The result was an American foreign policy skeptical of diplomacy and fearful of treaties that subordinated constitutional freedoms. Jefferson offered the strongest opposition to federalist ideas of a strong and forceful central government and executive powers. He decried secrecy and any policy that would subvert civil liberties and the provisions of the constitution.   Jefferson articulated avoidance of war as his foreign policy's primary goal; one that protected capitalism, but that based on America's abundant resources and self-reliance saw little need for foreign treaties and alliances.

Jeffersonians are first and foremost the protector of civil liberties and prosperity, however, focused inwardly on America domestic interests. Jeffersonian tenants were rooted in America's unique heritage and values, wrested with its rejection of European forms of government. Jefferson like many early American leaders was skeptical of diplomacy and foreign policies that would entangle and confine United States interests with unsavory allies. He believed that the United States was unique, and that the American Revolution was a "new era of the world". [11]

Jefferson, as a foreign delegate to France, was uniquely positioned to assess their respective revolutions. The French revolution evolved from a country in a state of collapse; the American Revolution occurred in the midst of peace and prosperity. The two revolutions may have had common republican objectives and the rejection of royalty, but in execution and result the French version of revolution was grossly different. The very nature of American rebellion and rejection of British tyranny was an

9

indictment of British, if not all European forms of government, while the French revolution was far more populist and dangerous, advocating the overthrow their monarchy and imparting political power to the people.[12] The French and the American revolutions similarly changed the manner in which both countries operated, both domestically and abroad. But Jefferson did not believe the French had duplicated the American example of republican government. The American form of democracy was culturally removed from Europe, and Jefferson did not advocate exporting the American brand of democracy as part of United States foreign policy.

As the first Secretary of State under George Washington, Jefferson's sentiments were nevertheless French. He advocated support for the French, but advised no involvement in their war with Great Britain. Jefferson, Washington, and John Quincy Adams were eloquent in their statements respecting the independence of other nations while asserting and maintaining America's independence. They were the early isolationists, if not pacifists. Washington cautioned against foreign entanglements,[13] and Adams would later advise that America "goes not abroad, in search of monsters to destroy. She is the well-wisher to the freedom and independence of all. She is the champion and vindicator only of her own."[14]

Jefferson thought war should be the last resort for what he considered obvious economic and social reasons. He believed preventing war was accomplished by defining American interests in narrow terms, "as an economy of means".[15] He believed in the patient use of negotiation, arbitration and sanctions to attain reasonable results; and if war is required it must be limited by the least possible application of force. Jefferson would use limited navy power to against the Barbary Pirates and later against the British, leading up to the War of 1812. Jefferson believed the costs of war created an undue reliance on a powerful centralized government. He cautioned against a large standing military, arguing that it would create socially oppressive centers of economic and political power.[16]

Jeffersonian non-interventionist ideas would play a large part in American foreign policy through World War I. Often seen as pacifists and principled isolationists,[17] presidential administrations, through World War I, would adopt Jeffersonian ideas. With the exception of the Civil War, the United States would avoid the ravages of war that would plague Europe throughout the 19th century. Successive presidents would shun entanglements and treaties that would abrogate constitutional liberties and lead to war. It was not until the United States began to grow as an industrial might that its foreign policy evolved to secure her destiny as a global economic power.

The Hamiltonian Tradition: Gunboat Diplomacy

The Hamiltonian tradition represents the more pragmatic, realist and capitalistic tenants of American foreign policy. Alexander Hamilton was the first United States Secretary of the Treasury and author of the Federalist Papers. He was the philosophical leader of the nationalist wing during the Constitutional Debates. Hamilton, a believer in a strong central government, was less concerned about individual freedoms. As seen by his opposition to the inclusion of the Bill of Rights, later the first ten Amendments to the Constitution, he believed individual freedoms were protected by the power invested in each separate state, and therefore not a necessary component of the Constitution. Hamilton failed to sustain the argument against the relentless affirmation of Thomas Jefferson and other civil libertarians.

Hamiltonians, drawing from American economic values, believed there was a fundamental link between commerce and government; that it was vital to the economic well being of the United States. Hamiltonians believe that the United States should compete in the global economy on the most favorable terms, and that this above all else drives the success of the American system.[18] The Hamiltonian tradition of Foreign Policy took form during the constitutional debates and again during George Washington's administration. Alexander Hamilton was foremost of the founding fathers to articulate commerce as a national interest. American liberty, capitalist values and geographic realities predated Hamilton and were largely the fundamental underpinnings leading to America's subsequent revolution and independence from Great Britain. It was entirely predictable that commerce, freedom, and access to trade and trading partners would have a great impact on United States Foreign Policy. Hamilton's views of "Continental realism" were far from isolationist, calling instead for an aggressive approach to statesmanship and foreign policy to ensure both economic and expansionist national interests. Hamiltonians, as Walter Reed describes, projected the uniquely American capitalist and independent values on other foreign governments. He believed that other counties like America would "consider their national interests, assess the ways and means of meeting those ends, and develop domestic and foreign policy in concert to achieve those ends."[19]

The Hamiltonian tradition takes a pragmatic view of intervention in world affairs, particularly when American commerce was threatened. Hamilton did not believe that America's abundance of resources and capital was sufficient to unilaterally sustain its economic growth. America would have to conduct commerce and trade with other nations. Foreseeing commerce as a vital national interest, Hamilton advocated for explicit government support of commercial centers of power. He advocated for a strong Navy to protect freedom of navigation and commerce. While Jefferson would argue for tariffs; Hamilton was against any economic treaties that might controvert domestic opportunity. Hamilton saw international commerce as a win-win strategy as opposed to a zero-sum game of war.[20] Jefferson would argue against central banks and a large standing navy and army, contending that they would assuredly lead to high levels of national debt that would ultimately compete with individual requirements for capital. Hamilton would suggest, otherwise; that far from a necessary evil, a strong central government supporting a large capitalist base was a critical requirement for American individual prosperity and economic power.

Hamiltonian defense of American economic interests is the basis for what many in the world sees as America's need for economic hegemony and military dominance. When critics of America charge that we are a colonial or imperial power, they refer to our past and present reliance on military power, particularly our naval might to ensure economic interests. The Hamiltonian tradition introduced *gunboat diplomacy* to our foreign policy lexicon, symbolizing America's industry and military power.[21] Hamilton's legacy explains the pragmatic diplomatic and military support of the socially oppressive governments Saudi Arabia and Kuwait, in large part to protect America's economic interests, particularly our reliance on the cheap and reliable flow of oil. Current United States realist foreign policy proponents; those projecting and defending American economic interests, gravitate from the Hamiltonian tradition of foreign policy.

The Jacksonian Tradition: Pride and Honor

The Jacksonian tradition, named after the military hero and 7th president, Andrew Jackson represents the more hawkish, populist and nationalist wings of American foreign policy. As Walter Mead explains, the Jacksonian tradition captures the American core warrior values; American self-reliance, code of equality and individualism.[22] Jacksonian tenants encapsulate America native and folk culture, its defense of community, if not its fighting spirit. Jacksonian tenants are instinctual, grounded in tribal and nationalist views. Jacksonians exploit nationalist pride and fervor and apply it to their foreign policy decisions.

Jacksonians join with the Jeffersonian tradition, however, believing in small government, states' rights and a hands-off approach on economics. Like Jeffersonians, they are skeptical of diplomacy and the prospects foreign intervention. Jacksonians and Jeffersonians however are more often at odds, reflecting the extremes in liberal and neo-conservatism policy. Jeffersonians would protect United States citizens through nonintervention, diplomacy and negotiation. Jacksonians advocate for a strong and aggressive use of national power implementing policies often opposed by Jeffersonians as obtrusive, arbitrary and constitutional.

Americans, individually have strong Jacksonian and nationalist views, particularly in times of war. They rarely appreciate appeasement and Presidents' put themselves and incredible political risk if they are perceived as weak in times of war.[23] Jacksonians are quick to understand and manipulate American fear, often used to gain support the application of military force. Jacksonians are for total war, particularly when rules are broken; above all when the United States has been attacked. As Walter Mead explains, "Jacksonians believe that there is an honor code in international life, as there was in

14

clan warfare in the borderlands of England, and those who live by the code will be treated under it. But those who violate the code, who commit terrorist acts against innocent civilians in peacetime for example, forfeit its protection and deserve no more consideration than rats."[24]

The Jacksonian legacy is seen today in the application executive power in both domestic policy and foreign policy. Many of our greatest liberal and progressive presidents have resorted to Jacksonian tenants when faced with war, resulting in success, but occasionally dishonorable results. Jacksonians or Federalists, fearing and expecting war with the French, passed the Alien and Sedition Acts 1798; acts designed to protect Americans and the government from internal and alien attack. President Jefferson would later repeal the Sedition Act, opposing its heavy handed use of executive power as an infringement of the personal and civil liberties. President Lincoln suspended of the writ of habeas corpus, allowing the military to arrest and detain American citizens suspected of subversive acts or speech. President Roosevelt authorized the interment of thousands of Japanese American's on the pretext that they posed a threat to national security. George Bush justified the Patriot Act in Jacksonian terms, arguing that these broader powers of the executive branch would be used to monitor, track and arrest suspected terrorists (aliens), enemies in the United States. When presidents resort to strategic bombing, mutual assured destruction, wars of attrition and "Shock and Awe", they speak with the Jacksonian clarity of purpose.[25] Jacksonians delineate victory as the end state, and that lasting peace is better served by the destruction on enemy forces and unconditional surrender of the opposing government.

The Wilsonian Tradition: Liberal Internationalism

      The Jeffersonian and Jacksonians traditions dominated American politics and foreign policy through the Civil War. But as America expanded west, and its economic strength and interests grew successive presidential applied largely Hamiltonian economic and Jeffersonian non-interventionist foreign policy. At the start of the 20th century, the United States rivaled Europe as an economic, scientific and industrial power. Americans participated, if not took the lead, during the Progressive Era, as automobiles, aeronautics, radio, electricity and advances in medicine changed their lives forever. Domestically, progressives advocated a wide range of economic, political, social, and moral reforms, as federal, state and local lawmakers debated the rights of workers, suffrage and other progressive policies.[26]

      Internationally, American presidents protected national interests through diplomacy and on only the rarest occasions the use of military force. United States foreign policy was considered self-centered if not isolationist. While its diplomacy was not always successful, the United States did not find itself involved in foreign wars that punctuated the 19th century. With the United States intervention into World War I, and in step with progressive domestic transformation, a far more idealistic and interventionist foreign policy emerged; the Wilsonian era of foreign policy.

      The Wilsonian Tradition of foreign policy is named after the 28th President, embraced the revolutionary ideas of liberal internationalism . European Leadership, with the exception of Germany, joined with President Wilson in supporting treaties and organizations designed to prevent the repetition of World War I, the "War to end all wars." President Wilson, after successfully intervening in World War I, vigorously defended ratification of the Versailles Peace Treaty and United States membership in the League of Nations. His ideas of liberal internationalism represented a distinct departure from the isolationist, economic and warrior-like aspects; tenants of the Jeffersonian, Hamilton and Jacksonian traditions.

> Our isolation was ended twenty years ago…. There can be no question of our ceasing to be a world power. The only question is whether we can refuse the moral leadership that is offered us, where we shall accept or reject the confidence of the world.[27]

Faced with Senate opposition to the America's membership in the League of Nations, Wilson questioned their motives, and in broader terms the motives of American interests. Wilson was adamant that America's participation and leadership was critical to establishing the League of Nations as a collective security organization that if successful would prevent war. Membership in the League, the "new world order", would ensure and extend self-determination and democracy beyond America and Europe, and punish nations for their aggressive nature.

Senate republicans opposed the Treaty and the League of Nations. Led by Henry Cabot Lodge of Massachusetts, they opposed the Versailles Treaty in Jeffersonian terms. Lodge agreed that the United States was the world's best hope, but argued that accepting the treaty and membership in the League of Nations, United States interests would be subordinated to the league and entangle America in the intrigues of Europe. Senator Cabot believed membership in a community of countries would impede America's ability to unilaterally "do good" and endanger her very existence. Lodge held Jefferson's view that Americans were unique, strong and generous. He was confident that if left unfettered Americans would act nobly to serve mankind. Lodge argued in cultural terms, when he cautioned that membership would trifle with America's "marvelous inheritance; this great land of ordered liberty."[28] The

Senate rejected the treaty and refused membership in the League of Nations. Woodrow Wilson's later unwillingness to compromise on the Treaty of Versailles after the First World War was considered one of the greatest presidential blunders.[29]

President Wilson's idea of world order and international cooperation were far too progressive for his domestic audience, but instead resonated with Europeans. Wilson believed that democratic governments were for the most part stable, less prone to rapid reversals in leadership and policy; more centered and rational in fermenting their national interests; and far less likely to be dominated by military elite. He believed that democracies rarely went to war with other democracies and more likely to move toward increasing degrees of moral and political agreement.[30] He offered a reverse argument as well; that totalitarian, corrupt and cruel authoritarian regimes make for untrustworthy partners in the pursuit of world peace.[31] By supporting democracies, Wilson defined national interests in international terms. Wilson would receive the Nobel Peace Prize in 1919 for his international views and peace-making efforts; his legacy would live on as the Wilsonian tradition of American foreign policy.

The Wilsonian tradition, as an extension of western democratic values, supports international law and security, economic development, social progress and human rights as key components for achieving world peace. Wilsonian foreign policy advocates for the protection and expansion of democracy and representative governments, as the best method to prevent world wars, and by extension, protect United States interests. The Wilsonian tradition, like the Hamiltonian, does not shy away from interventionist foreign policy. Wilsonian principles support intervention and if absolutely necessary war in pursuing international interests. Wilsonians believe in global economic imperatives; defending freedom of the seas, air, space and now cyberspace and the global environment. "They view United States foreign policy far beyond preconceived notions of national self-interest and security and including America's ethical obligations to the global community." [32]

The debate rages in the early twenty-first century, as Wilson's legacy and tradition are viewed in the context of decisions made by Presidents George Bush and Barrack Obama. Many believe President Bush's goal of democratization in Afghanistan and Iraq were a natural extension of Wilson's tradition and legacy. Other's claim the Bush doctrine was unilateral and absolutist; that regardless of its support of democratic governance, it certainly was not liberal or progressive, and therefore not a legitimate heir of Wilson's legacy. They point to the Bush Doctrine idea of United States primacy with its reliance on unilateral action, regime change, preventative and preemptive war as entirely juxtaposed and a perversion of the Wilsonian tradition. And now as President Obama has decided to dramatically increase troop strength in Afghanistan, he is seen by many as continuing George Bush's legacy.

The Wilsonian Tradition: Post WWII through 9-11

President Wilson was unsuccessful in his attempt to ratify the Treaty of Versailles, and the United States subsequently would not join the League of Nations. During the intervening years, marked by a world-wide depression and as tensions rose in Europe, the United States returned to its previously held isolationist foreign policy stance. However, in response to Japan's attack on Pearl Harbor and Germany's declaration of war, Roosevelt responded in Jacksonian and forceful terms. America responded to its loss in pride, honor and blood with acts of war, only redeemed by the unconditional surrender of Germany and Japan. Following World War II, the United

States and the Soviet Union became dominate and competing world superpowers, marking the end of American isolationist policies. Wilson's vision was realized. Twenty-one years after Wilson's death, President Truman would vindicate Wilson's vision and legacy by joining 50 other nations in creating of the United Nations.

The Wilsonian tradition since World War II has dominated United States foreign policy. Every president since Wilson has "embraced the core precepts of Wilsonianism. Nixon himself hung Wilson's portrait in the White House Cabinet Room. American Presidents Roosevelt, Kennedy, Clinton and now Bush have made the championing of democracy and freedom the centerpiece of their foreign policies."[33] In the aftermath of 9/11, America's interventionist foreign policy, if anything, has taken on even greater vitality.[34]

Immediately following World War II, President Truman introduced his doctrine and grand strategy, applying military, economic and diplomatic power to rebuild and secure Europe and Japan and defend against an emerging Soviet threat. The Truman Doctrine set the conditions for the Cold War, introducing *containment* and later *deterrence* to the lexicon of foreign policy. Truman's containment policy included a variety of military, economic, and diplomatic strategies to forestall the spread of Communism, enhancing America's security and influence abroad. The United States and the Soviets would compete as super powers, but only through their proxies engage in military conflict; the "dirty little wars" of the second half of the 20th century.[35] Both countries would agree to nuclear deterrence and the concept of Mutual Assured Destruction (MAD). While not expressly Wilsonian, MAD was ironically, seen by many as having not only prevented nuclear war, but conventional conflict between the Cold War superpowers.[36]

Later as liberal and conservative administrations continued to implement their versions of the Wilsonian tradition, they debated and differed drastically on their ethical responsibilities and the reality of global challenges. Jeffersonian and Jacksonian foreign policy tenants reemerged as successive presidents defined where and when military power was acceptable. The Kennedy and Johnson administrations reflected a combination of both Wilsonian interventionalism and Jacksonian military forcefulness, in their support of the South Vietnamese government. Alternatively, President Carter would share a Nobel Peace Prize for his diplomacy and patient negotiation, bringing hope and peace, if only for a short time, to the Middle-east.

President Reagan's foreign policy of "constructive engagement" was designed to nudge authoritarian regimes into the more socially progressive and liberal democratic governments.[37] His policies were responsible in large part, for the collapse of more authoritarian regimes in the Philippines, South Korea, South Africa, Central America, and the Soviet Union. Most critics would sustain Reagan's military support of the Mujahedeen in Afghanistan, but harshly criticize his political and military intervention in Central America.

During President George H. W. Bush's administration the Berlin Wall fell, marking the end of the Cold War. The United States emerged as the single remaining super power. Across the world, many looked to the United States for leadership. The perilous balance of power with the Soviets maintained by "mutual assured destruction" during the Cold War had passed, now replaced by, nationalism, genocide, environmental degradation and nuclear terrorism. The challenges and threats to the United States as the world's single remaining super power were daunting.[38] The United States was expected to deliver on its moral obligation to work in concert with the United Nations as protectors and guardians of humanity.

America's international leadership was soon tested, when Iraq invaded Kuwait, further threatening Saudi Arabia and western access to Middle Eastern oil. President George H. W. Bush would lead a multilateral, diplomatic and military response in to Saddam's invasion of Kuwait. Bush justified military action in Wilsonian, Jacksonian, and Hamiltonian terms; articulating American interests as international interests and the defense of a sovereign nation; as a means to punish Saddam's brutal and unwarranted attack; and finally as protecting economic interests; access to middle-eastern oil.

During Bush's administration the world witnessed the fall of the Soviet Empire and the dissolution of the Warsaw Pact. Millions of people experienced the freedom of democratic governance for the first time. However, while many were lifted out of poverty in Western Europe, millions more were subjugated to regional war, ethnic cleansing and genocide. At the end of his term, President Bush deployed the military in support, as part of a United Nations coalition supporting humanitarian efforts in Somalia.

President Clinton, inheriting Bush's intervention in Somalia, amended the humanitarian mission, adding nation-building to the formidable task. Clinton's change of mission, involved American forces in Somalia's civil-war, resulting in the dramatic loss of 18 soldiers, a political defeat for the Clinton Administration, repudiation of America's meddling in the domestic affairs of another nation. America's intervention in Somalia and subsequent early departure, for all its merit, was seen by most as a dismal failure.

As an application of military power, terrorists such as Osama Bin Laden took heart, believing America did not have the political or military staying power, when confronted by irregular forces employing asymmetric tactics. Clinton realigned America's interventionist military and foreign policy. Clinton would later declare that the "United States would henceforth concentrate on its domestic economic problems and withdraw from many foreign-policy leadership roles that it had customarily assumed… the United States would defer more to the United Nations and to our allies, and take a pass on dealing forcefully with the various middleweight powers that threaten us in the post-Cold War era."[39] But once having accepted the mantle as the world's single remaining super power, President Clinton and America was unable to shake its responsibilities; first in Haiti and later the Balkans.

President Clinton, in 1994, in conjunction with a United Nations trade embargo, intervened in Haiti, deploying 20,000 troops to restore the Aristide Presidency. When the United Nations arms embargo and peace keepers failed in preventing mass atrocities and genocide in Bosnia Herzegovina, President Clinton responded in both Wilsonian and Jacksonian terms. President Clinton first intervened with substantial military force expelling Serbians form Bosnia and Herzegovina and again later in Kosovo. Critics of President Clinton's foreign policy would claim the United States was slow in reacting to Yugoslavia's wars of dissolution, and subsequent genocide.[40] And ironically, he again was criticized for his use of strategic bombing campaign forcing the Serbians to capitulate in Kosovo.[41] Clinton improved upon Wilson's peaceful legacy with the application massive military force; first prevent further bloodshed; and second with the installation of democracy in Bosnia and Srpska to prevent a repetition of civil war.

Europe's failure to deal with ostensibly a European problem exposed their inability to effectively deal with their own regional problems.   Neo-conservatives in the United States argued the primacy of Unites States military might; that neither United Nations nor NATO had the requisite political will or military capability required maintaining regional, no less world peace. As the 21st century began, the proliferation of rogue nations with nuclear aspirations, non-state actors with religious and extremist ideologies, would challenge western democracies and world stability. The conditions were set for the next evolution in American foreign policy; the dominant and unilateral application of United States military force.

The Bush Presidency: "Going it Alone" in the Face of Terrorism

Candidate George W. Bush made President Clinton's interventionist foreign policy a primary campaign issue. Bush suggested he would pursue a "humble" foreign policy that would avoid the entanglements of the Bill Clinton years.[42] During the debates with Vice President Gore, Bush reiterated his belief that the America would only intervene with troops when our United States vital interests were at stake. "The mission must be clear. Soldiers must understand why we're going. The force must be strong enough so that the mission can be accomplished. And the exit strategy needs to be well-defined. I'm concerned that we're over deployed around the world… There may be some moments when we use our troops as peacekeepers, but not often."[43]

President Bush's foreign early policy was in line with his campaign theme; he was not interested in continuing Clinton's interventionist foreign policy, even as he inherited operations in the Balkans. The terrorist attacks of September 11, 2001 however, brought terrorism to the American homeland and a dramatic change in President Bush's foreign and domestic policies.   President Bush's foreign policy not only became interventionist but singularly unilateralist. Bush's "go-it-alone policy" was apparent when the United States invaded Afghanistan and quickly defeating the Taliban. President Bush's decisiveness, combined with early military success, calmed both domestic and foreign fears. The world accepted the United States invasion as its unilateral right to defend itself. This was not the case with Iraq. America's preemptive invasion of Iraq, the second use of unilateral action, alarmed and offended some United States allies, bolstering the view among many countries that America was an arrogant bully on the world stage.[44]

President Bush applied both sides of a United Nations-based argument. As a pretext for the invasion of Iraq, President Bush used Saddam Hussein's failure to comply with the international procedural processes, namely United Nations Security Council Resolutions 687 and 1441, requiring Iraq to destroy all chemical, nuclear and biological weapons. However, President Bush did not at the same time request a United Nations resolution supporting the invasion. President Bush justified the invasion of Iraq substantively in preventive terms; focusing on Iraq's past and expected future use of Weapons of Mass Destruction; and to prevent Iraq from replacing Afghanistan as Al Qaeda's next safe haven.   The United States coordinated and received strong military support from Great Britain and Australia; habitual American allies and by the Poland's Operational Maneuver Reconnaissance Group (GROM). However, the United States again did not seek multilateral or international procedural support. Many of those countries who provided military support the United States did so with very little political domestic support.[45]

After initial conventional success on the ground in 2003, the War in Iraq transitioned to one of national-building. Over the next four years the US, her Allies and the Iraq Security Forces defended the country against a determined insurgency. Subsequently, in 2008 the United States surged ground troops in Iraq. The surge provided adequate security that when combined an Iraqi population unwilling to tolerate terrorist attacks, successfully defeated the insurgents. Unfortunately, the success in Iraq was disquieted by a resurgence of a Taliban-based insurgency in Afghanistan. President Bush, left office in January, 2009 and would not see the successful culmination of events in Iraq and Afghanistan. President Bush, much like his predecessors, would leave his successor, in this case President Obama, with ongoing military operations, and no foreign policy solutions adequate to the America's role as the sole remaining superpower.

The Obama Presidency: The Prospect for World Peace

President Obama and the Democratic Party's recent victory in the 2008 election were seen by many as an indictment of President Bush's domestic and foreign policies. Whether considering foreign policy, the economy, jobs or health care, "Americans come out of this election with a heightened set of expectations of ending war, enlarging the economic pie for all and expanding the social safety nets provided by the government."[46] But now as President, what is his Grand Strategy; his foreign policy; his application of military force? The 1986 Goldwater-Nichols Act requires the publication of a National Security Strategy by June 15 of a new administration. As of this writing the Obama Administration had not published its first National Security Strategy. This paper

26

concludes with an analysis of President Obama's speeches as the best indicator of his foreign policy and Grand Strategy.

In his most recent and important speeches, his Nobel Peace Prize acceptance speech and his speech at the United States Military Academy at West Point, both in December, 2009, President Obama articulated his approach to foreign policy and application of military force. President Obama articulated, not as some have suggested, a politically motivated middle ground , but in the broader context, a centered and reflective mix of the realist and idealist wings of foreign policy that have historically transcended political parties and partisan politics.

> Our overarching goal remains the same: to disrupt, dismantle and defeat al-Qaeda in Afghanistan and Pakistan, and to prevent its capacity to threaten America and our allies in the future.[47]

President Obama spoke to the cadets of the United States Military Academy, justifying his decision to send an additional 30,000 troops to Afghanistan. Obama, ironically, continued and extended President Bush's Afghanistan strategy; departing from Bush's policy by establishing an end-state and directing the United States military to begin the transfer of our forces out of Afghanistan in July of 2011. His decision, in some respects, vindicated George Bush's invasion of Afghanistan, agreeing for the most part with Bush's foreign policy and the use and application of military power. Not surprisingly, President Obama's Afghanistan strategy pleased supporters of the war and dismayed many of his fellow liberal politicians and constituents. Fellow Democrat, Rep. Maxine Waters spoke for many liberals when on "Countdown Tonight with Keith Olbermann" she remarked that she was "I'm very saddened" by Obama's decision.[48] War critics had roundly condemned George W. Bush's justification of his invasion of Iraq; a preventive war to destroy Saddam's Weapons of Mass Destruction and to

27

prevent Al Qaeda from using Iraq as and training and staging ground. President

Obama justified his Afghan war strategy, similarly in preventive terms; escalating the

war in Afghanistan to prevent that war-torn country from again becoming "a staging

platform for terrorists."[49] But as one Obama liberal critic sadly states "The Bush regime

has expired in the United States. But under the Bush-Obama doctrine, America remains

committed to fighting perpetual wars for an elusive and ill-defined peace."[50]

> I know there is nothing weak -nothing passive - nothing naïve - in the creed and lives of Gandhi and King. But as a head of state sworn to protect and defend my nation, I cannot be guided by their examples alone…. For make no mistake: evil does exist in the world. A non-violent movement could not have halted Hitler's armies. Negotiations cannot convince al Qaeda's leaders to lay down their arms.[51]

This excerpt from President Obama's Nobel Peace Prize acceptance speech

was again, strikingly similar to his predecessor, George Bush's view of the world.

President Bush, in his 2002 State of the Union speech, stated "We've come to know

truths that we will never question: Evil is real, and it must be opposed."[52] Like President

Bush, Obama stressed the existence of evil and the repudiation of negotiation as

alternative to the use of force. President Obama's speech was a mix of idealism and

realism. Obama first praised the peaceful idealism of Martin Luther King Jr. and

Gandhi, but reasserted his sworn responsibility as America President to protect United

States interests, liberty and freedom. President Obama further articulated the

requirement for war and the unilateral use of force; "that the instruments of war do have

a role to play in preserving the peace" and further; "like any head of state - reserve the

right to act unilaterally if necessary to defend my nation."[53] President Obama assured

his audience that in a world in which "threats are more diffuse, and missions more

complex,"[54] the United States would focus on developing international political and military support; however if required, America would continue to act, alone if necessary, to protect its vital interests. Obama's Nobel Lecture may very well have been the most pro-war speech every given by a recipient of the Nobel Peace Prize. President Obama could have considered a Jeffersonian approach, rejecting the surge in Afghanistan, signaling his repudiation of regime change and war as a method to regress terrorism. But like American presidents before him, President Obama was not betting his legacy entirely on a diplomatic or softer approach to foreign affairs. His decision to escalate troops in Afghanistan, in Jacksonian terms, belies the clarity of purpose provided by the use of the military to protect or enhance America's vital national interests. His strategic narrative, clearly defined the use of diplomacy-first foreign policy approach and a multi-lateral view in implementing military force. President Obama made no apologies for the United States as the preeminent leader in global affairs. He communicated a hard truth; "The United States of America has helped underwrite global security for more than six decades with the blood of our citizens and the strength of our arms... we will not eradicate violent conflict in our lifetimes."[55] President Obama clearly intends to use military force, even as he continues to articulate a soft-power approach to foreign affairs.

Conclusion: A Measured Response to Terrorism

It is clear that American foreign policy is indeed unique, deeply rooted by its values, derived from its distinctive colonial heritage, geography, economic abundance and national experience. As America grew, its foreign policy evolved from one focused on isolation and protection to limited internationalism in support of commerce and trade. As the United States emerged as a world power, America's foreign policy dramatically

29

changed, reflecting Wilson's views of international liberalism with goal of achieving of world peace through the spread of democracy.

America faces a world unsettled by emerging regional powers, rogue states, non-state actors and global terrorism. Terrorist attacks aimed at the United States, strike at our democratic heritage, freedoms and liberty. President Obama should employ all forms of national power to preempt terrorist attacks, and if necessary, respond when America is attacked. Our domestic response should not include policies that infringe upon our constitutionally protected liberties, accomplishing for the terrorists what they cannot otherwise accomplish by their physical attacks on our homeland. Terrorism, especially when targeting civilians, has rarely if ever achieved the terrorists' stated goals and objectives. The United States only succeeds in response to terrorist threats by absorbing its effects and responding in realistic and appropriate means. Deviating from the rule of law and human rights gives terrorists the legitimacy they crave, but certainly do not deserve. The United States demonstrates its true strength by its uncompromising adherence to its values and by measured foreign policy in response to terrorist attacks.

The United States must return to multilateral responses to defeat terrorism. Our reaction should avoid unilateral action, even when understood and justified in light of our distinctive heritage and national experience. The United States cannot continue to rely on the Jacksonian view that large-scale military action, preventative war, and regime change are appropriate and reliable responses to terrorist attacks. Overreaction in foreign policy and the application of force, as we have seen in our recent conflicts, has provided terrorists with a moral equivalency. The pre-invasion bombing, urban area-clearing tactics, mistreatment and alleged torture provides the basis for future terrorist recruitment and support.

President Obama is now adjusting his foreign policy to protect America's blood and treasure. His stated purpose in the current conflicts, over the next two years, is to remove the bulk of our military forces from Iraq and Afghanistan. He is beginning to develop and communicate a strategic narrative that explains the military and diplomatic mistakes of the past administrations, while at the same time acknowledging the price in blood and honor, this country and underwritten in support of global peace. President Obama can focus world scrutiny and condemnation on terrorists and their sponsors. By keeping the focus on the terrorists, through our foreign policy, as reflected or of our unique heritage and place in the world, we can undermine the terrorist narrative of hate and disunity. The terrorist message of hate, though tactically their source of strength fundamentally undermines their ideology. Maintaining and moral high ground, based the American endearing culture and values, is the best foreign policy to bring about peace and prosperity at home and to the troubled parts of the world.

Endnotes

[1] Roger S. Whitcom, *The American Approach to Foreign Affairs*, (Praeger Publishers, 2001), 41.

[2] Samuel Rawson Gardiner, *The First Two Stuarts and the Puritan Revolution*, (New York: C. Scribner's Sons), 10–11.

[3] Whitcom, *The American Approach to Foreign Affairs*, 9.

[4] Ibid., 15

[5] Ibid., 10.

[6] Ibid., 21.

[7] Thomas Jefferson, "First Inaugural Address", Washington, D.C., March 4, 1801.

[8] David Fromkin, "Entangling Alliance," *Foreign Affairs*, July 1970, http://www.foreignaffairs.com/articles/24183/david-fromkin/entangling-alliances (accessed Jan 9, 2010).

[9] Walter R Mead, *Special Providence*, (Alfred A. Knoph, New York. 2002)

[10] Ibid., 99 – 263.

[11] Ibid., 180.

[12] Thomas Jefferson, "Letter to William Short", January 3, 1793, Thomas Jefferson Papers at the Library of Congress, http://chnm.gmu.edu/revolution/d/592/ (assessed Jan 25, 2010)

[13] George Washington, "Washington's Farewell Address", 1796, The Avalon Project, Yale University Law School, http://avalon.law.yale.edu/18th_century/washing.asp, (assessed Jan 22, 2010).

[14] John Quincy Adams, "Speech to the US House of Representatives on Foreign Policy", July 4, 1821, Miller Center for Public Affairs web page, University of Virginia, http://millercenter.org/scripps/archive/speeches/detail/3484, (assessed Jan 10, 2010).

[15] Mead, *Special Providence*, 194.

[16] Ibid., 197.

[17] Jason Ralph, "What Exactly is the Jeffersonian Tradition in US foreign Policy?", March 26, 2008, International Studies Association, 49th Annual Convention, Bridging Multiple Divides, Hilton San Francisco, San Francisco, CA, USA, http://www.allacademic.com/meta/p253816_index.html, (accessed Jan 05, 2010).

[18] Mead, Walter R., "Hamilton's Way," *World Policy Journal*, no. 13 (Fall 1996): 89-106.

[19] Mead, *Special Providence*, 100.

[20] Ibid., 103.

[21] Michel Pugh, "Is Mahan Still Alive? State Naval Power in the International System," *The Journal of Conflict Studies*, 17, no. 2, (Fall 1996), http://www.lib.unb.ca/Texts/JCS/bin/get.cgi?directory=J97/articles/&filename=pugh1.htm (accessed Jan 11, 2010).

[22] Mead, *Special Providence*, 102.

[23] Ibid., 221.

[24] David Talbot, "The making of a hawk, From Kuwait to Kosovo to Kabul, American firepower has been on the right side of history. The odyssey of a former dove," *Salon Magazine* (January 2, 2002), http://www.salon.com/books/feature/2002/01/03/hawk/index.html (accessed Jan 10, 2010).

[25] Ibid.

[26] John Whiteclay Chambers II, *The Tyranny of Change: America in the Progressive Era, 1890-1920*, (Rutgers University Press, 2000), 26-45.

[27] Woodrow Wilson, "Speech Given to the United States Senate America's Membership in the League of Nations", Washington, D.C., June 10th, 1919.

[28] Henry Cabot Lodge, Sr. "Speech Given to the United States Senate Against the League of Nations", Washington, D.C., August 12, 1919.

[29] "Scholars, Public Disagree On Worst Presidential Mistake", *University of Louisville the McConnell Center Web Page*, February 17, 2006, http://php.louisville.edu/news/news.php?news=533 (accessed Jan 5, 2010) .

[30] Mead, *Special Providence*, 162-163.

[31] G. John Ikenberry et al., *The Crisis of American Foreign Policy, Wilsonianism in the Twenty-first Century*, (Princeton University Press (November 24, 2008), 53.

[32] Sally, Steenland et al., "Pursuing the Global Common Good, Principle and Practice in US Foreign Policy", *The Center for American Progress*, 2007, www.americanprogress.org/issues/2007/10/pdf/PursuingGCG.pdf, (accessed Jan 21, 2010).

[33] Ibid., 5.

[34] David M. Kennedy, "What 'W' Owes to 'WW': President Bush May Not Even Know It, but He Can Trace His View of the World to Woodrow Wilson, Who Defined a Diplomatic Destiny for America That We Can't Escape", *The Atlantic Monthly* 295. Issue: 2. (March 2005): 36.

[35] Frank A. Ninkovich, *Modernity and Power: A History of the Domino Theory in the Twentieth Century*, (The University of Chicago Press, 1994), 245-248.

[36] Robert Jarvis, "Mutual Assured Destruction", *Foreign Policy*, no. 33 (Nov./Dec. 2002): 40-2.

[37] Toney Smith, "Wilsonianism", *American Foreign Relations Web Page*, 2010, http://www.americanforeignrelations.com/O-W/Wilsonianism.html, (accessed Jan 25, 2010).

[38] Steenland, "Pursuing the Global Common Good," 7.

[39] Elizabeth Pond, "Kosovo: Catalyst for Europe", *The Washington Quarterly*, (Autumn 1999), 77–92.

[40] "The Clinton doctrine - Bill Clinton's failed policies toward Bosnia-Herzegovina – Editorial", *National Review*, (June 21, 1993), http://findarticles.com/p/articles/mi_m1282/is_n12_v45/ai_13952916/?tag=content;col1 (accessed Jan 25, 2010).

[41] The Democratic Party, "Republicans Criticized Clinton During Kosovo Conflict," http://www.democrats.org/pdfs/gop_kosovo.pdf (accessed Jan 25, 2010).

[42] Romesh Ratnesar, "The End of Cowboy Diplomacy," *Time Magazine*, (Jul. 09, 2006), http://www.time.com/time/magazine/article/0,9171,1211578,00.html#ixzz0dIrBxa7z (accessed December 22, 2009).

[43] George W. Bush, "October 17, 2000 Debate Transcript," *Commission of Presidential Debates Web Page*, October 17, 2000, http://www.debates.org/index.php?page=october-17-2000-debate-transcript (accessed December 22, 2009).

[44] George W. Bush, "Going It Alone on Foreign Policy, Sept. 11 Response Seen as Illustrating Bush's Unilateralism," *National Public Radio Web Page*, http://www.npr.org/news/specials/091102reflections/foreign_policy/index.html (accessed December 22, 2009).

[45] Pew Research Center for the People & the Press, "A Year After Iraq War Mistrust of America in Europe Ever Higher, Muslim Anger Persists," March 16, 2004, http://people-press.org/report/206/a-year-after-iraq-war (accessed December 22, 2009).

[46] Waughn Ververs, "A Mandate For Change", *CBS News*, November 5, 2009, http://www.cbsnews.com/stories/2008/11/05/politics/main4572553.shtml (accessed January 08, 2010).

[47] Barrack Obama, "The Way Forward in Afghanistan and Pakistan," Eisenhower Hall Theatre, United States Military Academy at West Point, West Point, NY, December 1, 2009, http://www.whitehouse.gov/the-press-office/remarks-president-address-nation-way-forward-afghanistan-and-pakistan (accessed December 3, 2009).

[48] Joan Walsh, "Yes, It's Obama's War Now," *Salon Magazine*, (December 1, 2009), http://www.salon.com/news/afghanistan/index.html?story=/opinion/walsh/politics/2009/12/01/afghanistan_speech (accessed January 8, 2010.)

[49] George Will, "This Will Not End Well," *The Washington Post*, (December 2, 2009).

[50] Jack Kenny, "GOP Hawks Love Obama's War Talk," *The New American*, (December 18, 2009), http://www.thenewamerican.com/index.php/opinion/959-jack-kenny/2590-gop-hawks-love-obamas-war-talk (accessed January 8, 2010).

[51] Barrack Obama, "Nobel Lecture in the Oslo City Hall," *Nobel Prize Organization Web Page*, (December 10, 2009), http://nobelprize.org/nobel_prizes/peace/laureates/2009/obama-lecture_en.html (accessed December 28, 2009).

[52] George W. Bush, "2002 State of the Union Speech," *CNN*, (January 29, 2002), http://transcripts.cnn.com/2002/ALLPOLITICS/01/29/bush.speech.txt (accessed January 10, 2010).

[53] Obama, "Nobel Lecture"

[54] Ibid.

[55] Ibid.